Jesus and Ernie

Sue Mueller

ISBN 979-8-88751-928-9 (paperback)
ISBN 979-8-88751-929-6 (digital)

Christian Faith Publishing
832 Park Avenue
Meadville, PA 16335
www.christianfaithpublishing.com

Printed in the United States of America

If Jesus Had a Dog
The Final Years

Chapter 1

Jesus and I were on one of our walks when we ended up down by the water. There were a lot of people around. Jesus went into the water. His cousin, John, was there, and he poured water over Him. There was a big commotion in the sky, and I heard a voice saying, "This is My beloved son. Hear Him." I looked around but couldn't see anyone. I was very confused.

When Jesus came out of the water, He scratched behind my ears, and I knew everything was okay. He told me He was going into the desert for a short time, and I would stay home and keep Mother Mary company.

He was gone for a long time. It was forty long days. Mother Mary was doing a great job of taking care of me. She would talk with me and take me on walks. But not as long as the walks I would take with Jesus.

I missed Him. At night, I would cuddle up to her, and she would smile. She always gave me peace, and I would fall asleep at her feet.

When Jesus finally came home, I was so excited. I know I was being annoying, but I couldn't help it. I wanted Him to keep rubbing my ears and playing with me. He laughed. He never got angry with me.

While walking in the garden one morning, Jesus told me we were going to go to a party that day.

Not working in the workshop that day! Wow! That was unusual. The only day we didn't work in the workshop was on the Sabbath.

But a *party*! I was excited. That meant *food*. I was always good with that.

He said we were going with Mary and some of His friends. He had a lot of friends. People were very drawn to Jesus. Ever since we were down by the water and met Peter and his brother, Andrew, and James and his brother, John, we were together a lot. They gave up fishing and were bringing more and more people to listen to Jesus. He told wonderful stories about His Father in heaven.

We went to the party. They were celebrating a wedding. Weddings were a big time for parties. The food was great, and people danced. It would go on for a long time.

As the day went on, Mary came to Jesus and said they were running out of wine. Jesus asked what concern was this of His. But Mary went and told the servants to "Do whatever He tells you."

The servants seemed confused, but when Jesus told them to fill their wine jugs with water, they did it. Then He told them to fill a cup and bring it to the chief steward.

The chief steward was surprised when he tasted it and went to the groom and said that the good wine was usually served first, and when everyone had had their fill, the other wine was served. But they saved the best wine for last.

Wait! What! The water was changed to wine! I watched that water, and nobody did anything to it. But the water was changed to wine. Jesus had done something so amazing. It saved the bride and groom from an embarrassing moment.

After this, there was no stopping the crowds from coming to Jesus. Everywhere we went, people were coming to have Him cure their illnesses. People that were blind could now see. People who were sick were healed. Others who couldn't walk were now walking.

Once when we arrived in town, His friend, Lazarus, had died a few days before. His sisters Martha and Mary were very sad.

We went to the tomb, and Jesus called Lazarus, *and he came out!* People were really excited about that, especially his sisters, Martha and Mary. People were so happy. Jesus always made the people around Him happy.

Miracles were happening everywhere we went. But not everyone was happy. There were some from the temple that didn't like Him. They kept saying bad things about Jesus, which caused a commotion.

When that would happen, we would just leave that town. There were many other people that wanted to hear Him. We traveled around a lot.

Then there was the time we were on a mountain, and so many people were there. Jesus told His friends to feed all the people because they were hungry. They told Him they only had a few fish and a few loaves of bread.

But Jesus had the people sit down, and He blessed the food. It was enough to feed the thousands of people that were there. I had my fill too. And there was food left over.

Jesus had not only filled everyone's tummies but their hearts as well. He had filled them with love for Him and His heavenly Father.

He told them of the mercy of His heavenly Father and how they only needed to come and ask for forgiveness for their sins and live a good and holy life, helping one another and sharing this good news with others. It was a message of love to everyone.

Chapter 2

Last Days

My legs were not as strong as they used to be. Jesus usually walked a little slower for me. My body didn't always do what I wanted it to do. I couldn't run or jump anymore. Sometimes, Jesus would stop and rest so I could catch my breath, or we would take shorter walks.

Today, we all walked into town, but Jesus rode on a donkey.

People shouted and laid palm branches before us. I thought it was wonderful. They cheered for Jesus. I always knew He was great, but to see everyone giving Him praise made me feel proud to be His friend.

It was going to be a wonderful life with people knowing how great He was. Everyone wanted to be around Him.

That is why I didn't understand that only a few days later, everything changed. It started out okay. We had a special feast. I really enjoyed the dinner. It was extra special. Jesus's friends were there. At least the close ones. One of them, Judas, left early. He was in a hurry.

Afterward, we all followed Jesus to the garden. Jesus went there often, and it was usually peaceful, but tonight was different. Something in the air wasn't right. Jesus left us to go by Himself to pray. He seemed very sad. We all fell asleep.

Jesus came back and woke us to tell us to pray. When He left us, we fell asleep again. I am good at taking naps. My body was getting old, and I didn't have much energy anymore, so I napped whenever I could.

All of a sudden, there was a commotion, and Judas brought some soldiers. He kissed Jesus's cheek, and the soldiers took Jesus away. I wanted to go with Him, but Jesus told me to go with John. I didn't want to. I wanted to go with Him. But John picked me up and carried me home. I was very upset. Where were they taking Him?

The next day, I went with John and Mother Mary, and another Mary to a hill. Jesus was there, but I hardly recognized Him. He was beaten and could hardly stand. He was carrying a cross.

They nailed Him to that cross. I whined and whimpered. It had to hurt, but Jesus didn't make a sound.

I lay down at the bottom of the cross. I wanted to be as close as possible to Him. I wanted to lick His wounds, but I couldn't reach them. I had never experienced such sadness.

We stayed there all afternoon. Jesus looked at me. He didn't have to say anything, but I could feel His pain.

Then He looked up and said, "Father, forgive them, for they know not what they do."

He always forgave people when they were mean or pushed Him in the streets. But this was *big*! These people hurt Him so badly. I wanted to hurt them back, but He was forgiving them. I whined and whimpered.

Then He said, "Father, into your hands, I commend My Spirit." And He died.

I was heartbroken. They took Him down from the cross and placed Him on Mother Mary's lap. I wanted to climb up there too. Many times, she held me on her lap, and it was so comforting, but now there was Jesus on her lap. It wouldn't bring Him back. But His friends gently took Him and laid Him in a tomb.

I was so exhausted. I had no energy. I was so drained. I couldn't even walk home. John carried me.

The next day, it was the Sabbath. I stayed with John and Mother Mary, and it was a very quiet and sad day. I couldn't even eat. That was very unusual for me. I could always eat.

But on Sunday, there were all kinds of noise. The other Mary came, and John and Mother Mary went with her to the place where they buried Jesus. I followed behind.

But Jesus wasn't there! They were saying He was alive. He rose from the dead. I was confused. Other people died, but they didn't come back, except Lazarus. Where was Jesus?

I used my nose to find His scent, but I couldn't find it anywhere. I could always find Him when we played hide-and-seek when He was young, but not today.

I felt so lost. I felt alone, even with Mother Mary and John around.

Then, all of a sudden, *I saw Jesus sitting on a rock*. I was overjoyed. I ran to Him and jumped up into His arms. He laughed, patted my head, and rubbed my ears. *He was back*!

I was so happy. He smiled and told me He was taking me home to be with Him…*forever*. I had so much energy that I hadn't felt in years. My legs felt strong again, and I could run and jump.

He said we were going to meet His Father in our new home. *I was finally going to meet His Father in heaven*!

About the Author

Sue was born in Queens, New York, and worked in Manhattan before becoming a stay-at-home mom. She moved to Allentown, Pennsylvania, with her husband and children.

Sue is a mother of five, grandmother of ten, and great-grandmother of three so far, with hopefully more to come. While staying active in her children's activities, she started a computer business. She also worked as a secretary at a church, as a massage therapist, and has volunteered at her church and other community organizations.

The family has traveled quite a bit. They camped across the country for five weeks twice with the kids. Since then, she and her husband have enjoyed traveling. She runs trips for her church. She knows people like to go places, and she likes to organize, so it seems like a natural way to go.

She also started a bereavement support group in her church. After the passing of her youngest son, she knew there was a need for people to have a safe place to grieve. When you share joy, it is multiplied. When you share grief, it is divided.

Children are so vulnerable and need a safe place, and there is no safer place than in our Lord's care.